Consulting Interview

How to Respond to TOP 28 Personal Experience Interview Questions

Martha Gage

ISBN: 9781093755015

CONTENTS

Foreword

Did you know that 33% of the time, an Interviewer knows whether or not they would like to hire you in the first 90 seconds of an interview?

It's true.

A third of the time your interview is really and truly done in the first 90 seconds. This means that your preparations are paramount. You need to go in there ready to give them the information that they need and to have your image cultivated carefully for success. Another useful fact, 50% of Interviewers believe you can be ruled-out as a candidate simply by the way you dressed, poor manners, or even the way you walked into the office for your interview.

Yikes!

Don't worry. Help with that is what you came here for and we've got you covered.

We've collected a treasure trove of tips and tricks that will ensure you will have everything you need in order to look and act your best and GET the job you are targeting. It just takes a little preparation on your part based on the information we will provide you and you'll be able to ace any interview. Ready to get started?

Good.

Let's start with our first chapter, Preparation facts and tips, and we'll build a foundation to get you ready for landing that job of your dreams!

Chapter 1 – Preparation Facts and Tips

Proper preparation can make all the difference when it comes to interviews. Interviewers remember the people who have done their homework ahead of time. Know the business you are applying to become a part of, and they will be much, much more likely to select you for that all-important second interview of. They might even hire you on the spot!

That said? How best should one prepare?

We're glad that you asked! A number of simple things may be done to be prepared for your interview. Here are a few to get you started:

Preparation for interviews

1. Practice questions in the mirror.

Knowing your interview questions is simply not enough. You will want to practice how you will answer in front of the mirror. Watch your body language. Smile. If you practice enough then you will look confident in your interview and make exactly the right impression.

2. Know the Company that you are applying for.

You want to work for a specific company? What do you know about them? They are taking the time to consider you, so be sure to show your appreciation by spending a day to learn a little about the business you could soon be part of. What type of business is it? When were they founded? Coming into an interview armed with this information shows that you are serious, and a little trivia can get you the career of a lifetime.

3. Know why this company is a good fit for you.

Why are you choosing this position? When you are asked you should be able to let them know exactly why you are the perfect fit for this position. If it's a customer service job, perhaps you are a good fit because you like people. If it's accounting, perhaps you are a math wizard. Know why you want this job and it will show when you are interviewing. Count on it.

4. Bring 5 copies of your resume.

Odds are that you will be interviewing with more than one person, so make sure that you can advertise! Who knows? Maybe the job you are applying for is not your future, but rather one that you were not aware of they are just itching to fill. Your resume is your footprint, be sure to leave lots of them so Interviewers know exactly where to find you.

5. Refresh your memory about your career history... you'll be asked about it.

More important than memorizing interview questions (we advise strongly that you memorize questions too!), being able to describe, in detail, exactly what your function was in previous positions is your ticket to that new job you want! How else will they know all your accomplishments? Spend a little time rehearsing your history in the mirror so you can deliver the goods with confidence. You'll be glad you did!

6. Get a good night's sleep.

It seems simple but often the simple truths are the ones that serve you the best. Staying up all night before an interview is a mistake. Be sure to get enough sleep the night before and you'll be refreshed and ready for the day to come.

7. What is your biggest weakness?

Don't fall for this one. It's a popular interview question but you don't need to panic. Talk about something that you are working on. 'I used to have a problem with speaking in public, but I've been practicing.' This is the sort of answer they are looking for.

8. Tell me about yourself.

Prepare a biography for yourself ahead of time. Where have you worked, what have you done? Start by listing your jobs on a piece of paper and then expand on each piece. Did you work with people? List that. Did you help others meet deadlines? List it. Bank on it. Sell yourself!

9. Prepare questions for THEM.

The Interviewers are going to ask you this. What questions do you have for them? Where is the company going in 10 years? What are your career prospects? Ask the others where they see themselves going within the company framework. Get a taste of your future.

10. Dress for Success (but don't overdo it)

Look nice for your interview. Plan in advance: do they want a full suit or business casual? Dress right for your interview or you are just wasting time!

Now that we have reviewed your preparations, let's go to our next chapter, 'Mistakes to avoid.' Some of them are simple but others are simply just easy to overlook if you aren't prepared. We'll help you to make sure that this doesn't happen. Let's proceed!

Chapter 2 – Mistakes to avoid

We've discussed some preparations to make for your interviews. Next, we would like to discuss some common mistakes you can avoid if you keep a level head on your shoulders. These mistakes happen all the time and they are easy to avoid. Let's discuss:

1. Don't bring up salary and benefits right away!

Bringing up salary concerns too early in an interview can put you at a disadvantage when negotiating and it's also poor form. Let them make you a job offer first. DO expect that there will be some questions about salary; however, and make sure you know the rate you are looking for so you can negotiate when the time is right.

2. Do not talk bad about previous employers – keep it professional.

Talking bad about previous employers is a huge no-no. For one thing, it's unprofessional. It also makes the person interviewing you wonder what exactly you might have to say about them if they hired you and things didn't work out. You can say things like, 'I didn't feel that position was a good match for me,' or 'I'm looking for a better fit for me with chances to grow,' and express well enough you didn't enjoy the previous workplace in this manner. Disparaging remarks are simply unprofessional so avoid them at all costs.

3. Turn off that Cell phone!

Mistakes happen. You don't want that stellar interview to turn sour when your custom ringtone comes on. Keeping your cell phone on gives the impression you have more important things to be doing than interviewing for your new career. Avoid this by simply turning it off. Unless your current position requires you to be on-call (in which case you can set the phone to vibrate and apologize if it goes off), it simply isn't worth what it could cost you.

4. 'On time' is LATE

Always try to arrive at work or a job interview with 20 minutes to spare. This gives you time to review your notes, grab some water, and ensures you will have ample time to fill out any preliminary information which an Interviewer might require. As far as bad first impressions go, being late is one of the biggies, so don't sabotage your chances before you've even said a word.

5. Read the company webpage before you go in.

That Company webpage has information that is useful to you. Familiarize yourself with as much as you can of the layout. This will help you to avoid asking any questions where the answers might have been fairly obvious with a little research. It can't hurt and taking the moments needed to learn about the company could be that extra edge that gets you the job!

6. Don't lie.

This is the information age and you should never forget that. If you lie about yourself during an interview, then you might be costing yourself a job unnecessarily. Background checks can quickly reveal a lot of things, so if there is a concern it is better to be truthful. The honesty will be appreciated and if you don't get the position this time then you won't have burned down any of your bridges.

7. Resist posting about your interview on Facebook.

When you get home, don't rush to post about your interview on Social Media. Remember what we said about the information age? Anything you write could be seen by someone in the company or gossiped about by a friend who already works there.

8. Don't get lost on a question, compose yourself.

If you feel like you are stuck on a particular question or that you are communicating poorly, be sure to stop yourself and compose your thoughts. Things you can say:

- 'I think I may have misinterpreted your question, could you rephrase it for me?'
- 'Would it be helpful for me to explain this again in another fashion?'

Don't let yourself ramble on if you get lost. Take a pause, get clarification, and start over.

Acknowledging mistakes makes you look better than pushing blindly on. Trust us.

9. Don't forget to ask the next steps after the interview.

When the interview is concluded, be sure to ask what to expect in the process. While they likely know already if they wish to hire you or not, there are steps to be taken in every interview process that can be time consuming. Asking for the next steps also shows them you are serious about your application and are hoping to move forward, so don't leave out this simple step.

10. Do not harass by email or phone.

No one is going to want to hire you if you irritate them. A simple thank-you email at the close of the interview can help to get you noticed. If you don't hear something within one week, send a single email the next week and then do not email or call again for at least 2 weeks. If they are interested then you will hear back from them, just be patient and give them a little space.

We have advised you how to prepare and what to avoid. Let's proceed to the meat of this information sandwich.

The questions!

We've got the TOP 28 Personal Experience Interview Questions listed and ready for you to review. Be sure to take some notes and personalize your answers based on the tips provided and you can be sure to interview with confidence.

Let's get started!

Chapter 3 – Question Themes

In this section we have our interview questions, divided into the various niches that they encompass. The categories and number of questions are as follows:

- Leading others (6 questions)
- Managing a Team conflict (6 questions)
- Managing a personal conflict (6 questions)
- Influencing others (4 questions)
- Overcoming Challenges (4 questions)
- Others (2 questions)

In this section you will be given information to help you to better understand and address these questions so that when you encounter them in an Interview you are prepared enough to answer with cool confidence. This can make or break an interview, so be sure to pay close attention to what we recommend and soon you will see the results for yourself.

Without further ado, let's get started!

Leading others

In this section of our Question themes, we will discuss questions about your existing (or potential) leadership skills. Companies have to be able to see the big picture, thus when they hire you for a specific position, the chances are they are also visualizing your potential within a company in the years to come. Companies invest a lot of time and money in your training and so this is, of course, a valid interest. Answering questions about your leadership abilities or your interest in their development can help Interviewers determine if the position you are interviewing for is 'just a job' for you or if it is your potential *career*. Here are some questions commonly encountered, along with advice on how you can answer them with confidence! Let's begin:

1. 'In what specific ways do you motivate your team members?'

Team motivation is an important subject. How do you inspire others to perform at their best? Do you hold performance competitions, such as with many Sales teams? Do you give regular feedback so they know which areas they are excelling in and which may be improved? Have some stories from your management or other leadership roles. If you have not yet performed in a leadership capacity, taking a little time to study motivational factors in the workplace can show you have the knowledge and just waiting for your chance at the helm. Here are a few examples:

- Setting expectations so that Team Members don't become overwhelmed.
- Setting Milestones to rate progress and keep work on schedule.
- Providing consistent, quality feedback and praise as required.

Example answer:

- *'One of the ways I motivate my Team is providing regular feedback on their performance. This includes consistent praise when it is noticed that they are going above and beyond and if there are areas where they can improve, I like to deliver it as a challenge rather than a negative comment. In my experience, this tends to inspire them rather than discourage and the productivity numbers have reflected this.'*

2. 'Two employees have left before the deadline of a large and important project. How would you change your leadership style and tactics to meet the upcoming deadline?'

Even the best-defined projects can run into issues. In your capacity as a Manager or Team Leader, think of some times when members of the team have left or become sick and unable to perform their part of the project. In general, your response to this could be:

- Initiating a Team meeting to assess new skill assignments.
- Utilizing your knowledge of Team Members skill and dependency levels to redistribute the work on your own.
- Begin taking progress updates at a more aggressive pace to ensure the project doesn't fall behind.

Example answer:

- *'I would change my leadership style by going into a more aggressive mode. This would consist of redistributing the work based on our quarterly skill assessments so those with extra experience in certain tasks will help take up the slack in those areas, increasing our pace. I would maintain that pace by changing the frequency of progress updates, collecting oral progress reports on a daily basis to make sure that everyone is on track.'*

3. 'How would you describe your leadership style?'

This is a good question to think about. Generally, you will want to tailor your answer to the type of business as-needed, but a good thing to focus on is letting them know that it is going to depend largely on the environment.

Example answers:

- *'My leadership style is standard in some ways, setting milestones in projects to assure that we stay on schedule, as well as setting company expectations for employees and ensuring they have what they need to work their best.'*

- *'I see myself as the type of leader that works with my team and has their backs 100%. My job is basically clearing out obstacles from their path during a project and making sure we are all on the same page.'*

4. 'Tell me about a time an idea of yours improved efficiency or the overall workplace environment in some way. How did you ensure proper implementation of this plan?'

The purpose of this question is to determine not only your level of innovation and creative thinking but also your management skills. So, think of a time when you developed a change that improved efficiency and how you implemented it. Let them know the change you made and how you convinced others this was the best way to proceed.

Example answer:

- *'Communications with sales and our tech support department were losing clients due to the lack of tech support availability during demonstrations or trial runs of the software. I spoke with team member's management from both sides and we all agreed that having a few techs on-call for demonstrations would help, as well as providing a little more technical training to the sales department with some of the best technicians so they could be prepared if tech resources were temporarily unavailable. This ended up improving our sales numbers and overall customer experience, as well as negating the 'Us against Them' mentality that was developing between the sales and tech departments.'*

5. 'Tell me about a time you took the lead in a team project. What was the outcome of the project?'

Tell a story about a time when you were leading a project that ended to your satisfaction. Advise how you delegated roles, established timelines, ensured updates were consistent, and that all required resources were available for your team members, but do it with your own style. Don't be afraid to let them know that your role was important to the success of the project. They want to know you are a leader, show them you are!

Example answer:

- *'Our Team leader became ill at a crucial time in a project we were doing for a client. I was asked to fill in his shoes and immediately contacted the customer by phone to introduce myself, advising the situation, and providing my direct phone number with the promise I would be handling things personally and would be available for them when they need me. I let them know we have the project mapped out and I would personally apprise them of progress to make sure they wouldn't have any worries. After this, I did exactly that, working with my teammates directly to keep everything on track and with the customer, to keep them happy.'*

6. 'How do you make decisions about the compensation of team members?'

A number of factors can determine who gets extra compensation when deciding amongst team members. Examples include:

- **Growth as a leader** – A strong leader can make all the difference in team productivity. This is something that must be considered when deciding compensation.
- **Utilize a Pay Grid** – A Pay Grid is a method of measuring growth in the workplace based on performance, experience, and other skills important in your company. It is generally done in steps, ensuring every employee gets a fair and focused compensation model.
- **Outstanding productivity** – If an employee is meeting and exceeding expectations constantly, this is another factor that one might consider.
- **Retention data for clients** – The numbers say it all and in the competitive markets of

today, this factor cannot be ignored. The company will want to do it's best to retain these talents.

Example answer:

- *'I would utilize a combination of our existing pay grid to ensure proper compensation, referencing our retention data as well to identify our up and coming stars or current workhorse employees that have done so much and deserve a little appreciation to reward and retain their efforts.'*

Managing a Team conflict

Managing conflicts in the workplace is very important, both on the level of the manager as well as the team members. A team that is spending its energy in the creation of friction rather than production can make things difficult for everyone involved in a project. Here are some questions that Interviewers may use with you to determine how you would or have gone about resolving team conflicts so that smooth productivity could be restored in your workplace environment. Remember, all these questions are important so you will want to know your answers beforehand. Be prepared, be confident, and be hired.

Let's discuss our questions on managing a team conflict and how they relate to you.

1. 'Have you ever had a team member who kept raising objections during projects?'

This is another tough personal experience question. Think of a time when you were working with a team and one member seemed to be constantly upset with how the project was going. How did you address this? Generally, in a situation like this, you will need more data. Using empathy, you can discuss the team members criticisms in private and attempt to determine if the issue is personal or professional. Perhaps they are having a rough time in their lives or maybe they just don't like their teammates or have a contrary personality. Very important as well... are their concerns valid? If they have been with the company and their specific field for some time, then it is quite possible there is some merit to their complaints. Describe a situation like this from your experience, including what you did to resolve the issue and what happened as a result of your actions.

Example answer:

- *'We had a team member with a lot of seniority who would always raise objections at the end of every team meeting when asked, 'does anyone else have something that they would like to address before we conclude this meeting?' It had started after his quarterly review and I had my suspicions about this and so I spoke with him privately. With a bit of discussion and an empathic approach I asked if his change in behavior had anything to do with the quarterly review. He said they did. He felt I had been overly critical in my review and that his seniority and contributions were not fully appreciated on the team. I let him know that my opinions were not meant to be negative, only as areas which could be improved upon, and spoke about good contributions I am personally aware he made over that quarter as well. The recognition and praise were all that was needed, it turned out, and the objections only came out when they were genuine for the rest of that quarter.'*

2. 'What is your preferred approach for helping employees to mediate/resolve a conflict?'

This will be a much more personalized answer as well, but we can give you an example. 'I prefer to mediate, obtaining information from both sides in an attempt to understand the issue. Once we've found some common ground, we can build on this from here and generally issues can be effectively resolved.' More important in this question are the details you will need to supply. How do you typically approach a situation like this? Do you set up a private meeting to discuss the facts? If so, do you speak with each one separately before engaging both in a private discussion? Do you get input from other team members who are not involved in, but may have their productivity affected by the conflict? All of this is important to showing your style of leadership, as mediation and empathy are powerful skills in a leader's tool chest.

Example answer:

- *'I prefer a direct mediation, meeting in a conference room with the employees who are having the conflict so we can talk it out. Everyone is allowed to speak for brief periods without interruption while we find a common ground so we can get things settled. Generally, just getting to finish what they wanted to say calms them enough to work together.'*

3. 'Tell me about a time you worked in a team and had to manage a conflict.'

This is a question you will hear a lot and is one you will want to answer carefully. What the Interviewer is doing is assessing your ability to creatively push through problems as well as your leadership abilities and your charisma as it relates to the management of others who are in a highly emotional state. If there are multiple Interviewers, you may get this question a second time, so we recommend you collect a few stories, rather than one, so when the Interviewers discuss you collectively there will be more points regarding your character to discuss. This can increase your chances of getting hired tremendously.

Your stories must include the following:

- A 'hook' statement describing the conflict situation in 20-30 seconds. Keep it brief and concise.
- Spend the rest of your story time (no more than 2 or 3 minutes) letting them know the actions you took to resolve the issue and the results.
- Emphasis on YOU, not the team. Do not be humble.

So, why are we structuring it this way? First, your opening statement is what catches their attention. Keeping it brief and concise shows you can summarize professionally, with no words wasted.

Next, we are spending most of the time following this statement with the actions you took, which demonstrates your creativity, ability to manage others, and your potential for the company should they hire you.

Lastly, we are emphasizing the 'I.' Yes, there is no 'I' in 'Team,' but remember they are evaluating YOU, not the team. Stick to this method and you'll look good every time.

Example answer:

- *'Two teammates who don't like each other were arguing about the most efficient way to fill our clients order. One preferred an expedited shipping method to meet our deadline and was more costly but would get the order there on time. The other argued the client was quite laid back and wouldn't mind a delay of a day or two and felt that the expedited shipping was cost prohibitive and useless in this scenario. I solved it by asking them to simply decide who would call the customer and ask them which method they preferred. The customer was fine with waiting a day or two and thanked us for giving that extra option to meet their deadline, stating it showed the commitment they have come to be used to from our company. Problem solved.'*

4. 'How would you advise a team member who complained about a coworker's behavior?'

Mediation can be a tricky subject. Without specific training the best one can do is empathize (but without taking sides, as this can create a worse conflict), so if you are not the team leader then be careful how you proceed. Some would choose to advise them to do their best to get their job done and that if this person is affecting their productivity, they should speak privately with their team leader. You could also remind them that the bottom line is trying to maintain a productive and healthy mentality for the workspace, but this is going to be a matter of personal style. Some might simply say, whichever answers are the best for you, practice them in front of a mirror so that your responses are firm, but warm.

Example answer:

- *'I understand that you are having a difficult time, but it is not my place to get involved in office politics, I'm just here to get the job done. If it's affecting your productivity, then it might be best to check with the team leader, but I would personally leave management out of it until I've spoken with the T.L. first.'*

5. 'How would you react if a coworker blamed you for something that wasn't entirely your fault (example, missing a deadline) during a meeting?'

How you behave when someone puts you on the spot is one of the things that can truly separate the amateurs from the professionals. Generally, you want your response to this sort of question to be along the lines of the listing below.

Example answer:

- *'I understand that you have some concerns about my performance which we disagree upon. Let's keep this professional and focus on our meeting for now and once we've completed this we can discuss our individual responsibilities further between ourselves or with our team leader present.'*

Keeping cool under criticism takes practice but it will never serve you wrong in the workplace. Jumping to an immediate defense can escalate a conflict and further disrupt the meeting, so it's best to make it clear you wish to address their concerns while also keeping the focus on your meeting.

6. 'You've noticed that a team member is arrogant or aggressive toward the rest of the team. How would you approach this person?'

If advising as a team leader this would definitely be something that needed to be addressed. First off, empathy is required. Maybe this person doesn't even realize that their behavior is any different from normal. As a team leader you might like to speak with them privately and try to discern if there are unspoken issues between them and the rest of the team and, if so, what the individual is specifically looking to have addressed. Maybe they didn't get a promotion or there has been previous friction with certain team members that might indicate another team would be a more productive fit for them. Each case is individual so as a rule, start with empathy and go from there.

Example answer:

- *'I would ask them to speak privately and start by praising points of their performance to get them ready for the 'medicine' part of the discussion, where I would ask if they knew they were coming across as being arrogant when this was likely not their intent. At this point, we could discern if the behavior was personality or purposeful and proceed as needed to get them working more fluidly with the team again.'*

Managing a personal conflict

Managing team conflicts are one thing but managing personal conflicts can be quite another. How you comport yourself when you are in the workplace around others can tell an Interviewer a lot of things about you. Are you good at managing others but have a hard time managing yourself? Is it the other way around? These questions are examples that you will hear in interviews, so, prepare in advance and be sure to approach answering them with confidence. Let's continue and we'll show you what we are talking about.

1. 'Tell me about a time when you had an issue with a co-worker.'

Everyone has had an issue with a co-worker. No matter who you are, someone has been difficult to work with at some point in your career. Likely more than one. What is important, however, is how you handle it, and this is what your Interviewer is going to ascertain. This is why it is good to prepare a few stories of this nature in advance, so that you can tell about a time when this occurred for you and what specific actions you took.

Example answers:

- *'I attempted to understand their side of the issue so that we could reach a common ground and get the work done.'*
- *'I simply talked with them and found out they were going through a difficult time right now. After that, we worked well*

together, sometimes it just takes a little empathy and patience.'

Of course, your answers are going to be specifically your own, but these can give you an idea.

What the Interviewer is looking for is to see if you are a team player and to know if you can handle a little diplomacy on your own and won't need to run to the manager for every disagreement. Collect a few stories of this nature, where you settled some issues on your own, and you are ready for this question in interviews.

2. 'Tell me about a time when you disagreed with your boss.'

Difficult at first glance to answer. Interviewers are looking to see if your decisions are data-driven, if you have the diplomacy to get them implemented, and if you are a team player when a conflict doesn't go your way. It's okay to disagree with your boss but it is very important how you approach it.

Example answer:

- *'During a project I found a way to quickly achieve an objective that we were coming to soon. My boss was hesitant to change our current strategy for achieving this objective. I asked for a private meeting and stated my reasons for wanting to implement this change, offering hard data showing why it could save us time and advising that I was more than happy to use either method to achieve our objective but wanted to bring this to his attention. When he saw the data, he agreed that my solution might indeed save us time and we communicated this change to the rest of the team.'*

Your boss is not inflexible and if you improve a process, by all means, speak up. That said, you must be willing to gather data to support your reasons but also be willing to perform a job the way that you have been instructed if your boss is not receptive to the change. Interviewers that ask this sort of question want to see how you deal with authority. When you select your story, keep in mind it doesn't have to be a time when you were right. Giving a story where it turned out that you were wrong, is also an acceptable answer as it shows that you focused on the job and willing to admit when you are wrong.

3. 'Are there any times where you had a conflict with a superior other than your boss? If yes, how did you handle it and resolve it?'

Another test of how you deal with authority. Proper answers to this will be similar but keep in mind we are now talking about a superior from another department. Think of a time when you were working with another team or department and the team leader or manager disagreed with an approach you wanted to take to completing a task or filling an order. What did you do?

Example answer:

- *'I was working on a technical issue with a security appliance that my client had purchased. We had to escalate the case, as we did not have the tools necessary to mitigate the issue. It had been escalated for a long time because that department was quite busy and due to the season, a number of employees were out sick. The client in question was one of our larger clients and sales were quite worried that we might lose their business. My manager, when asked, advised me to get creative. Working with sales, I took a list of escalated cases and sorted them by dates and by revenue. With this information, I wrote the escalation manager, copying my boss, and asked what can be done, as this client was one of our top 3 revenue-producing clients. The escalation manager, presented with this data, reallocated resources to help ensure we kept our client.'*

There are going to be times when you disagree with authority. Don't be afraid to tell a story about when you did this and what happened. Just focus on the communication you did, the diplomacy, the task, and its results.

4. 'How do you cope with conflict in the workplace?'

A more generalized version of the conflict question. How do you deal with general conflict in the workplace? Again, the focus here is going to be communication and not going straight to management when you have issues. Employers want to know that you can utilize diplomacy and deal with issues without disrupting the workflow.

Example answer:

- *'Communication, empathy, and a little common sense can help keep conflicts at bay in the workplace. I find that simply talking to the individual and trying to understand their side of the issue is generally the only thing required to stop a conflict from escalating. Management has more important things to deal with.'*

Answers like these help demonstrate that you deal with such issues on your own.

5. 'How do you deal with angry customers who complain about your products/services?'

This question evaluates not only your conflict resolution but your customer service soft skills as well. The first rule of dealing with an angry customer is to let them talk with as little interruption as possible. Generally, a customer wants to know you are listening and if you keep interrupting then things can escalate. When they are slowing down, show what empathy that you can. Let them know you understand their issue, repeat what they have told you in their own words, and let them know you will pass along their feedback. So, in synopsis:

- Don't interrupt!
- Show empathy for the customer.
- Repeat what they have said in their own words.
- Advise that you will pass along feedback.

Your personal stories will vary, of course, based on your department, compensation options that you might have had for the customers, and other personal variables, but this gives you a good foundation on how to tailor your answer to this question.

Example answer:

- *'First I let them talk without interruption. When they start losing steam, I empathize with them, letting them know I understand they are frustrated and that we were sorry this contact had to be under such circumstances. I'd advise that we are passing on their feedback and if they see any issues like this again to contact me personally. This generally calms most customers down.'*

6. 'What would you do if your manager gave you negative feedback on the way you approached a problem?'

This is a scenario where your Interviewer is trying to see how you handle criticism and to determine whether you took it as negativity or as a chance to improve your performance and to learn more about what is expected of you. In a case such as this, you want to be truthful. Let them know a time that someone was not happy with your work, how you reacted, and what changes you made to improve it.

Example answer:

- *'My boss told me my reports on a specific project were disorganized. She said I might want to try creating a spreadsheet to communicate the results. I thanked her for the feedback and said I would give it a try. The spreadsheet method was actually so good that we used it for many projects going forward.'*

Some things that you should NOT do when answering this question:

- Do not make up a story. Managers are quite good at sniffing it out if you are faking it. You'll probably be noticed and subsequently not hired.
- Don't say you have never received negative feedback. Everyone has. If you have to look a little deeper at your employment history, then take some time to do it. Everyone makes

mistakes, it is a primary means of how we learn.

- Don't go into excessive details on your slip up, just focus on what you did to improve things.

Follow these do's and don'ts and you'll answer this question just fine.

Influencing others

So, you've been asked about leadership, conflict, and other potential aspects about the job. What about your personal charisma? How do you get people to work effectively with you on getting something done? In this section, we'll go through some questions which address this and give you the recommendations you need to custom-tailor the perfect answers. Are you ready? Here we go:

1. 'Do you consider yourself to be a leader or a follower?'

This is another tricky question. The answer you will want to give is that you are BOTH. In the workplace there are times when you have to buckle-down and focus completely on the workload; however, there are other times when a snap-decision is required, and you are the only one that can make that call. Examples of what you can say:

- Talk about times that you took charge when it was needed.
- Mention times when you had to be both a leader and a follower.
- Advise of skills that you have sharpened, which are useful to both leader and follower; such as diplomacy, work prioritization, or organizational skills.

Avoid stating you are only a leader. While you might think this is what they wish to hear, it is not. The interviewers want to know that you may be relied upon to perform your tasks as needed but you also have the confidence to make a difficult call if that is what is required. This ensures you can be the type of employee that will stay and grow with the company.

Example answer:

- *'I consider myself both a leader and a follower. I follow my job directives and milestones and if I am needed to take action, I lead by example or direct decisions.'*

2. 'What do you do to influence team members on a project?'

Every leadership style is a matter of personal preference. What sort of strategies do you employ? While we don't generally make a structured list of the things we do at work, here are some tips that can help remind you (or empower you, if you have not had much experience in influencing teams).

- Be consistent, to build a reputation with your team as being reliable.
- Build trust with your coworkers through work and being personable.
- Listen to your coworker's suggestions and they will listen to yours.
- Know everyone's name and use it often. People appreciate recognition.

In a nutshell. You influence team members the most by being reliable, personable, trustworthy, and open-minded to the suggestions of others when attempting to accomplish a task as a team.

Example answer:

- *'I like to influence with my reputation for straightforwardness and reliability. I also listen to others and always call them by name; you'd be surprised how far that little practice goes.'*

3. *'Do you consider yourself to be an influencer?'*

This is a question that you can reply 'yes' to; but be humble. What they are asking is, are you a person that is good at handling people. Are you able to get people motivated to complete their tasks? Are you an influencer by the example of your performance and demeanor at work?

Examples answers:

- *'I would say that I influence by example, when not directly in a leadership role.'*
- *'In a leadership role, I am definitely an influencer. You have to be able to motivate and influence your team by milestones and examples.'*
- *'Only when I need to be to get the job done. In this capacity, I can influence customers to try new services or to retain them. I can influence team members by examples and directives.'*

Find something from your personal experience that applies to this. Everyone has had to sell an idea or motivate a coworker at some point in time. This is what they are looking to learn about you. Maybe you have the skills, but do you have the charisma? Tell them about your own experiences so they know that you DO.

4. 'How do you influence others to do what you want?'

Influencing others is an important leadership skill and, thus, how you answer this question can be a deal-breaker if you are not prepared. So, what do you do to influence others in the workplace? Do you share your ideas first with those who are receptive, so that you can gain interest in the changes you wish to implement or the tasks you wish to accomplish? Do you run your ideas by others in anticipation of earning their interest in the project through your request for input? You'll want to think on this subject so you can be prepared to show the Interviewers how you manage others. Other means of influence:

- Building trust: People are more likely to agree with you and cooperate if they trust in your vision.
- Being flexible: Be open to criticism or other ways of implementing your ideas.
- Be diligent: Don't let others see you 'napping,' always be pushing for the accomplishment of your goal.
- First one in, last one out: Some people always seem to be working. This is not very common so if this is you, be sure to mention it. Co-

workers see that sort of behavior and respect it, and this can be very influential in getting others to go that extra mile.

These are just a few examples for you to draw upon. You will have a number of your own you will find with a little reflection. Focus on what you do that makes others want to work with you instead of against you, and you can't go wrong answering this question.

Example answer:

- *'I influence others by building my reputation among them. First, as a hard worker, and someone they can trust. I listen to them as well and because of this and mutual respect, they listen to me.'*

Overcoming challenges

Your problem-solving skills are going to get you far in the work-place but you will need to draw attention to them. Interviewers have collections of questions, just such as these, that can help them discern what type of problem-solver you are, so they can make a better assessment of whether or not they wish to hire you and where they would like to place you. How you answer these questions is very important, so be sure to pay attention.

Let's begin:

1. 'Tell me About an Obstacle you overcame.'

While it seems like a maddening question, there is a very good reason you are being asked this. How do you behave when there is work to be done but there are problems in your way? Some tips on formulating your response include:

- The 'STAR' approach. This includes situation, task, approach, and result. Simply put, say what was happening, what you needed to accomplish (and the problem), what you tried, and the results. This is a good way to keep it simple and concise.
- Use an example that relates to the position you are interviewing for, if at all possible.
- Focus on your positivity: knowing that you keep good morale under pressure can help interviewers to make the right decision.
- Tell the truth. Don't pick examples where your involvement was minimal or completely

make something up. Managers will catch you at that quite quickly.

Example answer:

- *'We had a deadline approaching and 2 team members were out sick. I suggested that we set up a team meeting that afternoon and discuss our skill sets so we could divide the remaining tasks up among the rest of us. The meeting took a bit of time, but we were able to divide up the tasks and meet our deadline.'*

Your examples will have more detail and be more personal, but this gives you the gist of something basic you could say. Keep it simple but focus on how it was a stressful situation, and how you pulled everyone together so workplace objectives could be met.

2. *'Tell me about a time when you were challenged and made a mistake.'*

This question is very challenging. First, don't try to infer you never make mistakes, everyone does. Being able to speak about a time when you made a mistake with confidence shows that you are human, and you learn just like everyone else. Important tips to keep in mind when you are answering this question are as follows:

- No blaming: Blaming sounds like you are making an excuse and can make Interviewers feel that you are not confident enough in yourself to admit errors, should they occur. Avoid blaming when you tell your story.

- Focus on what you learned: What happened and what did it teach you? Is it something you still use to this day?
- What was the resolution to the problem?

All these items are good to include in your story. Employers will know that you can not only admit your mistakes, but you learn from them and retain the knowledge as you progress in your career path. It also shows decisiveness and strength of character, so be sure to work together some strong examples for this question so you will have something to say if asked.

Example answer:

- *'I was asked to make a training presentation on a software product that we work with. I was new to the office and not yet used to the pace of the environment and I realized I wasn't going to be able to finish the presentation at work and have it ready by the upcoming Monday. Thankfully, I was given permission to bring home the files that I need and do the work in my personal time but more importantly I learned a lesson in time-management. The training session got prepared and I was much more careful about how I allotted my task-time after that.'*

Gather a few examples of lessons where you have learned like this and this question will be a piece of cake!

3. 'What are some early workplace challenges that have served you the most?'

Interviewers may ask you this, in regard to some earlier challenges you experienced in your career. Don't worry, no tricks. This is simply another obstacle question you can ace with a little forethought. It is just another indicator of how you have faced a number of tricky issues throughout the years, and it is there to see some of what you have learned from it. They don't even have to be very complex. Examples could include:

- Learning to back up your work after a hard drive crash on your work computer.
- Learning that notes are still useful after forgetting a memorized speech you had to make.
- Learning how to take constructive criticism and use it to improve your performance, instead of letting it ruin your day.
- Learning that free training at work should always be taken advantage of (after seeing others get promoted).

These are just a few examples of small things that challenge us. As you can see, the answers don't always have to be complex. Small things that you pick up along the way indicate a lot about your character. So, find a few examples to have at the ready that went from 'momentary challenge' to life-long lesson.

Example answer:

- *'I had been working on a spreadsheet in order to track some metrics with other employees. The spreadsheet was networked, with all of us able to write to it during our opposing shifts. I didn't realize we didn't have individual spreadsheets and some corrections I made ended up causing problems with the spreadsheet's table. Once saved, we had to start over again. I advised my team leader I hadn't fully understood how to work in this manner and should have asked for a quick training session, offering to work some extra time without compensation to replace lost data. After that, I'm not afraid to ask for an explanation of how something works if I don't understand it. Productivity is worth more than pride.'*

4. 'What is the biggest challenge you ever had to face?'

This is a difficult question, but we can give you some guidelines on how to answer this properly. First, do NOT include personal challenges. Some of us have survived through some very tough personal times and while this is something to be proud of, this is not something that we want to bring into the interview. That said, if your biggest challenge was not an illness or tragedy, but say, learning mountain climbing, then you could talk about this. Interviewers are attempting to learn how you deal with adversity in the workplace; however, it is best, if possible, to memorize a good example from a challenge that happened there. Some tips about this:

- Keep your example just a few minutes in length.
- Try to keep it work related.
- If just out of college or you have very little work experience at this time, a thesis or athletic accomplishment works well.

Give it a bit of thought and be sure to rehearse your story in the mirror, so that you can deliver it with confidence.

Example answer:

- *'My biggest challenge was my first time as a manager. I'd been recommended for the position and really had no idea just how much was done behind the scenes to keep things running. I had to create schedules, manage conflicts, interface with angry or high-maintenance customers, and generally left work later than anyone else every day for a long time. I took to the challenge; however, doing some company management training in my free time and consulting other managers for tips on what to do. Soon the pace was more, well, 'manageable.' Now I realize that the coworker who referred me knew me a little better than I thought.'*

Other Questions

We also wanted to include two questions that are often asked you might not yet have prepared for. We're including them here so when you DO encounter them then you will be more than ready.

1. 'Why consulting?'

So, you have just been asked 'why consulting?' and wondering what to reply. Well, as you may or may not know by now, depending on your current experience level, there are a number of EXCELLENT reasons why one might choose to be a consultant. Here is an overview of the most popular:

a. Learn a variety of things in the field

One of the joys of consulting is that you will get to work with a variety of techniques and mediums within your field. This gives you exposure to a variety of means and methods to accomplish work in your field, often with the very latest of technology and trends that you simply couldn't accomplish easily in another job.

b. Fastest way to learn

Subsequently, as this exposure is hands-on, you will learn at a pace that students in a college can't compete with. This is one of the reasons that consultants are in demand. Why have lab experience when you can work with someone who has real-world experience? Consultants can typically work for 2-4 years and then generally begin working expert level jobs in their chosen field should they tire of consulting.

c. Make excellent contacts

Consultants gain contacts that can make all the difference in your career. For instance, they often work directly with CEO's and other high-level corporate operatives that someone working directly in the company might never meet (or have to spend years working up to meeting). They also can develop a network of other consultant experts that can prove quite lucrative when seeking future contracts or even starting a consulting firm.

d. Travel

Consultants are often required to travel, so if you are young and have wandering feet or older and tired of the tedium, Consulting can help you to scratch the travelling itch while helping you save a good amount of cash. Part of this is the fact that your travel expenses, including hotel and typically a food per diem are reimbursed or provided in advance for you.

e. Pay grade

This is included for your informational purposes, but this is one that you should not mention in your interview. Consultants tend to make much higher rates than standard workers in comparative fields. This is due to the travel and the flexibility that is required; however, the multiple benefits are certainly worth it.

f. Sometimes college assistance is offered

This is another benefit that likely should not be mentioned in your interview, unless you say, 'I enjoy consulting because quite often there are training programs which help me to improve my personal skill set.' That said, quite often consultants may be offered assistance in college training in order to add a degree to their existing practical expertise. It's quite a nice perk.

Example answer:

- *'I chose Consulting because I am serious in my field and willing to sacrifice remaining stationary and growing at a steady pace for the quick and explosive experience growth that consulting offers. I like working with a wide variety of technologies and methods in my field and a less variable job-path would limit my exposure to these. Consulting is simply the most sensible solution for me to accomplish this.'*

2. 'Why this firm?'

Our last question is probably the most important. Your Interviewer is asking you, 'Why us? Why are we a good fit for your future?' This is where our recommendation of getting to know the company is important. Think hard about this one and formulate a good answer. Do they have technologies you wish to work with? Are they a juggernaut, simply one of the best in an industry you admire or have been working in already? Maybe your research has indicated a high level of employee satisfaction and retention. These are all things you might want to cite if they apply.

Example answer:

- *'I chose this firm because it is one of the market leaders with a proven track record, a high level of employee happiness and retention, and because it sets many industry standards in my field. I feel like my dedication to this field would mean this firm is an excellent opportunity for me to thrive at the same time, I am working daily with others who are as dedicated, while doing the work I am good at and that I love.'*

Afterword

We'd like to thank you for your purchase of *Consulting Interview: How to Respond to TOP 28 Interview Questions*. We hope that you will take advantage of what you have learned to better understand these top questions that Interviewers will be using to assess you so you can ace that interview and get the job of your dreams.

Don't neglect the basics, such as learning more about the company for which you are applying, practicing your questions in the mirror, customizing your stories, and keeping them honest. After all, these Interviewers are interested in you, otherwise they wouldn't be giving you a foot in the door. Use your new interviewing skills to make sure they pull that door of opportunities open wide and let you in to your new career. It is waiting for you right now.

So, get yourself a coffee and find a comfortable spot, bring a notebook or your personal laptop computer, and get started drafting those question responses at your leisure. Memorize and recite them in the mirror until you know your body language and presentation voice-tones by heart. Then go get that job!

We know that you can do it!